MAKING ROOM FOR NEIGHBORS

Your Name Here

MAKING ROOM FOR NEIGHBORS

Finding Community in Your Backyard

Max Lucado and Randy Frazee

Making Room For Neighbors

Hendrickson Publishers Marketing, LLC
P. O. Box 3473
Peabody, Massachusetts 01961-3473

ISBN 978-1-59856-657-4

Published by arrangement with Oak Hills Church, San Antonio, Texas.

New curriculum prepared with the assistance of Brett Eastman at Lifetogether and Small Group Publishing. Resources previously published by Brett Eastman are adapted and used by permission.

Unless otherwise noted, all Scripture quotations are taken from THE MESSAGE. © 1993, 1994, 1995, 1996, 2000, 2001, 2002 by Eugene H. Peterson. Used by permission of NavPress Publishing Group.

Scripture quotations marked NIV are taken from the Holy Bible, New International Version®, NIV®. © 1973, 1978, 1984 by Biblica, Inc.™ Used by permission of Zondervan. All rights reserved worldwide. www.zondervan.com.

Printed in China

First Printing — December 2010

Table of Contents

INTRODUCTION

APPENDIX

LEADER NOTES

Acknowledgments

Andy Ivankovich
Executive Producer

Brett Eastman
Producer

Major Lytton
Director

Mark Tidwell
Executive Minister

Gerry True
Minister of Communications

Davida Lambert
Minister of Training Resources

Greg Ingram
Minister to Neighborhoods

DeLisa Ivy
Project Manager

Desmond Lewis
Coordinator

Tommy Owen
Design and Layout

Mike Bowie
Camera, Lighting, and Audio

Casey Friesenhahn
Gaffer/Grip

Jim Matthews
Camera, Lighting, and Audio

Neil Wilson
Copywriter

Max Lucado:
As always, and in new ways, Denalyn, you continue to be a partner beyond compare. I continue to learn what it means to grow in the art of hospitality by watching you. Thank you for always practicing it first and foremost with me.

Randy Frazee:
I'd like to thank my wife, Rozanne, and the rest of my family for their patience and support as we discovered the *Table* together. Without you I would have never seen all that God had planned. You are a blessing.

Special Thanks to Steve and Melinda McBride and Sandy and Rosa Roberts, who graciously opened your hearts and your homes so that others may be blessed. Your hospitality is clearly seen throughout this project. We love you guys!

Greetings

Life is short and days are busy . . . it's time for a real change of pace, a new look at the priorities, people, and places that fill our lives. Imagine a way of living that actually makes room for what we say is important! Imagine being able to relax at the end of a long day and say to yourself, *This is the way I always hoped life would be.*

Our aim with this *Making Room for Neighbors* series is that you will intentionally go deeper with your family and get more engaged with your personal relationships. Along the way, you may discover a few new friendships right in your backyard! It's time to discover that neighbors can be so much more than strangers we wave to in a friendly way.

Imagine a neighborhood gathering! Picture people around your table or fire pit, laughing and talking. Step up and actually do what we all think of putting into practice—getting connected with the people around us.

This curriculum is designed to be a catalyst to help you gather a few of your friends, families, and neighbors for an informal discussion about how to make room for life. It's really easy to do and a whole lot of fun. All you have to do is:

• Make a list of the families in your neighborhood that you think would enjoy or benefit from this experience.

• Call a few of them within the next 24 hours. You may even want to ask a few of them to help make this gathering happen.

• Host a neighbors' dessert or meal. Introduce the idea of meeting together throughout the year.

Our prayer is that your life is filled with grace, love, and joy beyond measure. Let's make room for neighbors together!

— *Randy & Max*

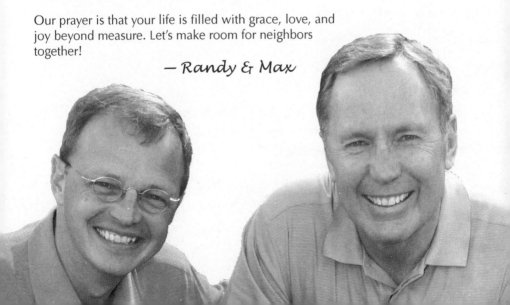

Introduction

Getting Started

Making Room for Neighbors says a lot with the title. It calls for commitment and change. That's where we start—not doing life the way we've done it before. We're going to break some old habits and hesitations and open our lives in new ways to others. We're going to discover the real people who live an arm's length from us. We're going to enjoy our neighbors next door and under our own roof.

This booklet and the video sessions that go with it cover five gatherings. But you can make these sessions spread out over several months as your group develops. This may be part of an ongoing group, or a yearly neighborhood gathering that runs for a season. Go through the sessions with the people you already know, and then plot out how you can get the whole neighborhood involved in another round of sessions.

Parts of Each Session

Each of the five sessions in *Making Room for Neighbors* has the same basic structure. We have tried to construct the gatherings so that they flow naturally from one part to the next. Below we've listed the titles for each of the session sections, with a brief explanation of each. Take a moment to read through the components of the sessions so you know how they flow together to create a group experience.

The Story Behind
This brief introduction at the beginning of each session allows you to see where things are going and provides some behind-the-scenes details that will sharpen your understanding of the personal accounts included in each session.

Coming Together

You've watched people get into a pool: some are toe-dippers, others start with a cannonball! These ice-breakers will give you a variety of chances to get to know the others in your group without having to risk too much. These are fun times with new people . . . even with ones you think you know!

Learning Together — Video

This 10- to 15-minute segment will introduce you to the main topic of the session and give you a real-life glimpse of the theme in someone's experience. It concludes with reflections by Randy and Rozanne Frazee and Max and Denalyn Lucado expanding on the theme of each session.

Notes

Some special notes from the teaching team and space to keep some notes for yourself.

Growing Together — Discussion Questions

These follow-up questions will allow you to add your own reflections, illustrations, stories, and insights into what you saw and heard during the video.

Deeper Bible Study

For groups who are ready to pursue an extended time of study together, these studies are designed to explore Bible passages that help us understand God's commitment to community and the other themes of *Making Room for Neighbors*.

Sharing Together

These are the action steps and gentle challenges of each session. The questions will encourage you to decide how you are going to live by these principles.

Hint for Next Time

A brief glimpse of the theme for the next session.

Other Useful Hints

Transitions

Encourage everyone to bring their booklets and keep them open as you follow along with each session. The point is not to rush through the components of the sessions—they are the means to the end of experiencing community.

Options

Use the questions as suggestions. As the group gets relaxed, you may want to expand the sessions to spend more time "chilling" (what you will rediscover in Session Four). Each of the sessions may take several gatherings.

Time Management

These are intended to be laid-back and relaxed sessions, but if you are facilitating, keep track of the time. Have a stopping point when people can have permission to leave. It's better to call it a night when things are still lively than to wait until everyone is looking for an exit!

Back Matter

Take some time to flip through the Appendix starting on page 60. There you'll find additional resources that will assist you in your efforts to make neighborhood gatherings a reality where you live.

Different Spiritual Maturities

Consider the background and spiritual experiences of your group. These sessions will draw people out, but not everyone will start from the same place. Give people permission to observe quietly if they don't feel they have anything to say, especially during the parts of the sessions that include Bible discussions. They will join when they are ready.

When to Use Making Room for Neighbors

The contents of this workbook and the accompanying DVD can be used in at least four different settings:

A. A small group primarily made up of Christians.
B. An adult church group looking for outreach resources.
C. A family interested in a home-centered life of faith.
D. An informal neighborhood gathering.

Customizing *Making Room for Neighbors* to your group:

Groups A and B (see description above) can use the materials as presented. Incorporating a study of Randy Frazee's book *Making Room for Life* for background and deeper application is highly encouraged. We recommend devoting a minimum of ten weeks to this study—a week for each session followed by a week for reporting and feedback on applying the previous week's lesson.

Group C can use the materials with the possible alteration of starting with Session 2: Making Room for Family. Adults and older children should participate in the study, but the entire family should be exposed to the application projects. This could be adopted as a year-long project by a family as a way of radically restructuring how they approach times together and their view of their surrounding neighborhood. Inclusion, as much as possible, of all family members will heighten the impact of the study. Again, parents would benefit from reading and discussing Randy's book *Making Room for Life*.

Group D would be one of the expected outcomes of the study by Groups A, B, and C. In the *Making Room for Neighbors* workbook you'll find good questions that will get people talking at a deeper level as well as guidance for hosts, leaders, and facilitators. On the DVD, many personal stories can be shown as a way to start discussion.

The *Making Room for Neighbors* DVD and workbook give you the benefit of years of experience from the Frazees, who have developed and practiced these principles in their neighborhood. It's a simple way to start (or continue) strengthening relationships and building community right in your own backyard. This program is not a "quick fix," but it will challenge and equip you to live out Jesus' command to "love your neighbor."

The greatest impact of *Making Room for Neighbors* will be in your own and your family's lives!

SESSION
ONE
making room for life

The Story Behind the Neighborhood

You've just seen Randy talk about his neighborhood gathering. The group that meets in his neighborhood is nearing 60 people. Although it took Randy and Rozanne over 14 months to develop relationships before their gatherings began, they knew from experience that true community can't be rushed. Randy has spent almost ten years using the neighborhood gathering model to strengthen communities of all kinds. Whether your neighborhood is large or small, urban or rural, this method is proven to work. Would you be willing to begin praying and taking practical steps to start fostering your own relationships with your neighbors? By hosting a barbecue or other neighborhood activities with the young and old alike, you will become better prepared to host your own neighborhood gatherings.

"As long as the earth endures, seedtime and harvest, cold and heat, summer and winter, day and night will never cease."
(Genesis 8:22, NIV)

Coming Together

If this is your first time together as a group, there are some important things to discuss. It's always fun to take some time getting to know one another. Does everyone know everyone else's name? Here are a few ideas you can use to break the ice as you begin this series.

1

My Best Year

Here you can take your choice: tell us about the best year you ever had and what made it special, or tell us what your dream vacation would be if there were no limitations (e.g., children, work, schedules, outside commitments).

2

How Did You Get Here?

Invite everyone to briefly share how they came to live in this neighborhood. Where did they move from and why did they decide on this little corner of the globe to establish a home?

3

My Immediate Neighborhood

On a large piece of paper or poster board, draw a simple map of your street with the five or six homes that are closest to yours. Label them with as many of the names of the people who live in each home as you can remember. Take time before the next session to fill in the blanks.

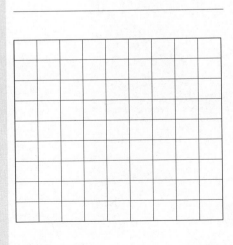

Roll Tape DVD Session 1

Learning Together (notes)

The section below provides you with some open space to write down your reactions, reflections, and resolutions based on the teaching and testimonies. As you listen, write down your thoughts and be prepared to discuss them later.

_____

_____

_____

_____

_____

Possible Components of a Neighborhood Gathering:

- Mingling
- Circling for prayer
- Sharing a meal
- Bible reading
- Praying over shared concerns
- Journaling the journey
- Planning for service opportunities

Action Step 1: Be intentional about how you approach neighbors.

Growing Together

Reflect on some of what you heard and saw during the video segments. Offer your thoughts to the group, using some or all of the following questions:

1 What is one new thing you want to start doing and one thing you want to stop doing in order to be more intentional this year?

2 Take a look at the three-month calendar located on the inside cover of the workbook. Take a moment to write down three to five calendar items. Commit to share these items with someone else a week from now.

3 What is one way you have been intentional with your neighbors in past years?

Deeper Bible Study

Your group may want to look at the biblical background of this session's emphasis on making room for a different schedule and realigned priorities this year. The following two passages allow us to think not only about Jesus in community, but also about the ways he taught his followers to view people around them.

S	M	T	W	T	F	S
		1 *small groups*	2	3	4	5
6	7	8	9 *ball game*	10	11	12
13	14	15 *small groups*	16	17	18	19
20	21	22	23	24 *vacation*	25	26
27	28	29 *small groups*	30			

Matthew 9:35–38 "Seeing the Neighborhood"

1 Jesus combined two different pictures into one when he looked at the crowds that came to be with him. What was the idea, and what does it mean to see people that way?

2 In what ways does your view of your immediate neighbors include the possibility that some of them are "found" and some of them are "lost"? What choices do these possibilities create for you?

3 How would praying for your neighbors by name and need begin to change the depth of your perception of them and your relationship with them?

See also Luke 19:41–44; Exodus 20:16–17.

Luke 24:13–35 "Hosting Jesus"

1 After walking and talking with Jesus on the road to Emmaus, what made the men invite Jesus to stay the evening? When you spend meaningful time with Jesus, do you tend to assume you're leaving him behind when it's over, or that you are taking him with you as you move on?

2 What distinct actions of Jesus did God use to open the eyes of the men who were hosting him in Emmaus? How do you recognize the signs that Jesus is working in your life or in someone else's life?

3 In what ways would you like to see your relationship with Jesus significantly change for the better this next year? What will those changes require from you?

See also Deuteronomy 6:4–9, 20–25.

Sharing Together

Suggestions for practical application based on the conversation of the session:

My Dreams
Take a moment to think about and then record below what you consider to be your three most significant dreams for reaching out to your neighborhood.

1._____

2._____

3._____

Discuss what should go on the Neighborhood Calendar on the inside front cover of this workbook (see the sample on page 17). Discuss ways you can "safeguard" certain dates, times, and occasions for the kinds of priorities Randy and Max are talking about.

Talk through the elements that Randy mentioned were part of the neighborhood gathering: mingling, circling for prayer, sharing a meal, Bible reading, praying over shared concerns, journaling the journey, and planning for service opportunities. Choose one or two of these to incorporate in this group as you go forward.

Hint for Next Time

If the whole idea of making significant lifestyle changes intrigues you, you might want to read Randy Frazee's book, *Making Room for Life*. It provides background for many of the concepts we will explore in these sessions. And the central idea that makes the other parts of this life project work is the *Table*, the subject of our next gathering.

Notes

_____

_____

_____

_____

_____

_____

_____

_____

_____

SESSION
TWO
making room for family

The Story Behind the Family Table

In an average neighborhood, people are always coming and going. For many people, being home is only a brief stop in a busy schedule. But here and there, some homes are different. Some families have decided it's time to do something counter-cultural. Instead of all the choices that pull people apart and keep them from experiencing any sense of community, this family has chosen to renew the age-old practice of the family table.

The ingredients aren't new: good food, time, table, and people. Like any good recipe, every ingredient is essential. The people who gather at the table may vary quite a bit, but

"Therefore, as we have opportunity, let us do good to all people, especially to those who belong to the family of believers."
(Galatians 6:10, NIV)

there must be a consistent core group. Whether it's a biological family or a family of faith, this core group will be transformed at the table. Once the power of the table affects their lives, gathering as a family becomes the unspoken priority. Only genuine crises or emergencies keep people from the table. Those who find themselves at the table for the first time are amazed that something so simple could leave them so deeply moved, accepted, and heard. These are not extraordinary people—just ordinary parents, children, and brothers and sisters in Christ who learn that the table is an effective tool for expression, for change, and for life itself. Will you come to the table?

Coming Together

If at all possible, arrange your gathering space so that your entire group is around a table. Whether it's a large table or a small table, a family room or kitchen table, a card table or a banquet, they all have one thing in common—they are places where people can gather.

1

My Most Unforgettable Table

Some meals just stick with you! Perhaps it's the setting (exotic or simple), or the surrounding events (graduation, engagement, retirement), or the participants. As you think over your life, what meals stand out to you as being candidates for your "Most Unforgettable Table" list? Take turns with your group sharing the stories of some of those meals.

2

Slow Food

We all know what fast food is, but what's your idea of slow food? Why has fast food become the norm in much of our society? What changes do you think might happen if more of us ate slow food?

3

Fun Facts

Give everyone a card and ask them to write down one fun fact about themselves that they are pretty sure no one else at the table knows. Collect the cards and shuffle them without looking. Read off the results one card at a time and invite the group to guess who wrote them. If the revelation provokes curious questions from the group, let the interaction flow for a while.

Roll Tape
DVD
Session 2

Learning Together (notes)

The section below provides you with some open space to write down your reactions, reflections, and resolutions based on the teaching and testimonies. As you listen, write down your thoughts and be prepared to discuss them later.

_____

_____

_____

_____

_____

_____

_____

_____

_____

_____

Learning Together

"One activity that would significantly improve your children's chances of normal passage into healthy adulthood: eating around the table five times a week."

5 Table Principles:

- One table
- Invite Jesus' presence
- Serve family style
- One conversation
- Festival of cleaning up

Growing Together

Take some time to talk about the teaching session. Reflect on some of what you heard and saw from Randy and the visit to the Frazee household. Offer your thoughts to the group, using some or all of the following questions:

1 What was one of your favorite memories around the dinner table?

2 What impressed or affected you the most as you observed the interaction around the Frazee family table?

3 The disciples of Jesus shared hundreds of meals with him. What do you think was memorable about sitting at a table with Jesus?

4 Review the five principles Randy shared that are essential components of an effective table experience. Which one surprised you the most? Why? Which ones do you know you need to intentionally incorporate in your own table gatherings?

Interview with Randy Frazee

Randy and Brett have an extended conversation about the central role of the *Table* that lies at the heart of this outreach emphasis. Discuss their points using your own questions or any of the ones listed on the top of the next page.

Brett & Randy

1 If you incorporated the idea of the table in your household, what difference would you expect it to make?

2 Comparing your situation to Randy's, do you think you're more likely to apply these lessons about the table out of necessity or out of vision? Why?

3 In what ways does the discussion we've had in this session impact the family and neighborhood dreams you identified in the last session?

Deeper Bible Study

As Randy points out, the table is a location that shows up repeatedly in the accounts of Jesus' life. He shared many meals with his disciples and others. The longest account of a single event in the Gospels has to do with Jesus' final meal with his disciples before going to the cross—the Last Supper (John 13–17). Below are two other passages that illustrate the way Jesus taught and how lives were changed in the vicinity of the table.

Luke 7:36–50 "More Than Food"

1 Who were the key participants in this event at the Pharisee's house? Why do you think Jesus was invited?

2 How did the woman acknowledge Jesus' presence in a unique way? When we invite Jesus to be present, how do our actions indicate that we believe he's there?

3 Why did Jesus forgive this woman's sins? How did the observers react to his mercy towards her?

4 How did Jesus focus the conversation at the table? Was this a good or bad thing? Why?

Matthew 9:9–13 "Who's Welcome?"

1 The first thing Matthew did when he began to follow Jesus was to open his house for a get-acquainted party. Who showed up at Matthew's house?

2 What made it possible for Jesus to be at home no matter whose company he was keeping?

{ _____ }

3 How do you think Matthew and his friends felt about Jesus joining the party?

{ _____ }

4 What was the point of Jesus' statement: "I'm after mercy, not religion" (Matthew 9:13)?

{ _____ }

Serving the Lord's Supper

Originally, the Lord's Supper was served at a table. During the early years of the church, Communion was usually part of a larger meal. But a table setting for Communion can add a significant intimacy for people who are used to receiving the elements in pews or even at the front of the church. Here you will need to be sensitive to the various backgrounds of the members of your group and your own comfort in sharing the elements.

Sharing Together

Suggestions for practical application based on the conversation of the session:

1 What table experiences have you had that fit some of the characteristics that Randy spoke about?

2 Which people on your block would you be willing to invite to your home for some kind of adventure in hospitality? When you think about coming to the table, who are you considering bringing with you?

3 How can we do a better job of being there for each other when our days are 9s as well as 2s?

4 What specific steps have you taken or are you taking to be more intentional, particularly when it comes to your family table?

Hint for Next Time

Now that we've looked at the *Table* as our base of operations, we will look next into our neighborhood to think about how we can reach those beyond our walls who have something to bring to our table and to receive from it.

Notes

SESSION
THREE
making room for neighbors

The Story Behind the Open Chair

Somewhere in your neighborhood there's a guy like Mark. When Randy Frazee thinks of Mark, the phrase that comes to his mind is "regular guy." Mark has lived on the same street for years. He doesn't avoid his neighbors, but he doesn't go out of his way to spend time with them, either. It just seems easier for everyone to mind their own business. Mark remembers walking the dog up and down the street several times each week, smiling and saying hello to his neighbors, but never having a conversation with the people who lived a stone's throw in every direction. His neighbors noted each other's presence, but they never lingered with each other.

"'Love others as well as you love yourself.' There is no other commandment that ranks with these."
(Mark 12:31)

Mark has always been a healthy guy, and one activity he enjoys is an almost daily ritual of bike riding. Like many people, Mark doesn't mind that others don't join him; he looks forward to it every day.

Something has been on Mark's mind lately, though. He's been hearing from his pastor that following Jesus eventually has a lot to do with one's flesh-and-blood neighbors, not the theoretical ones. As a result, a gradual change came into Mark's life. He didn't do that much to change his schedule, but he started living in a way that opened a door, or better, created an open chair for neighbors. During this session, we will learn what Mark discovered when he decided to offer an open chair to his neighbors.

Coming Together

This may be your third time together as a group, but each time needs a starting point, an attention-getter, to get everyone on the same page. Here are a couple of ideas you can use, if needed, to get the session going:

1

For the Memories We Make

Who has lived in the neighborhood the longest? Take a poll of the group and figure out when each family moved in. What memorable event happened in history that year that you can connect with that family's arrival here? Share memories of unusual events that are part of your neighborhood's history: the year the water main broke; the tornado, earthquake, or storm that caused major damage to several homes; mini-disasters that pulled people together.

2

For What's Mine Is Yours

Discuss as a group which people in the neighborhood have demonstrated special skills in home maintenance (be specific—who keeps their gutters the cleanest?), auto repair, painting, gardening, forestry, or gadget installation. Vote on who has the most unusual tool or mechanical device on your block. (Someone may own a 40-foot extension ladder or an unusual device for a homeowner to possess—like a Zamboni machine.)

3

For Such Time as This

What kind of schedule does your neighborhood live by? What events or activities like kids' sports teams, barbecues, holiday parties, etc., can serve as a reason to get together? Share your basic schedules and see what happens.

Learning Together

Roll Tape
DVD
Session 3

This three-part video presentation illustrates the wonder of discovering the open chair, the theme for this session. It includes an introduction with Randy and Max, followed by Mark's story, and then some reflections by Max and Denalyn Lucado on the basics of hospitality.

Learning Together (notes)

The section below provides you with some open space to write down your reactions, reflections, and resolutions based on the teaching and testimonies. As you listen, write down your thoughts and be prepared to discuss them later.

_____
_____
_____
_____
_____
_____
_____
_____
_____
_____

"Hospitality" and "hospital" are related words. They refer to a place of rest, recovery, refuge.

Reflections from Max and Denalyn on Hospitality

Circle the one that resonates with you most.

- We live lives that often end up looking like cocoons.

- It's not good for people to be alone, and yet we're surrounded by lonely people.

- Don't take your own healthy environment as the norm. Share it with others.

- Consider the block an extension of your home.

Max suggests three ways to demonstrate to your neighbors they are important and valuable:

1 Extend a personal invitation for contact: a dinner, party, or gathering.

2 Meet them at the door with a hearty "Welcome!"

3 When they leave, offer them a blessing. Speak good words into their lives. Offer to pray for them. Thank them for sharing their time.

As you listen to Max review these questions, who is God bringing to mind?_____

Growing Together

Now join the conversation between Max and Denalyn. Reflect on some of what you heard and saw during the video segments. Contribute your own comments using some or all of the following questions:

1 What struck you personally about Mark's story? How might you respond if one of your neighbors were sitting in the driveway with an empty lawn chair next to him or her?

2 In this neighborhood, what are some of the ways that we are practicing the things that neighbors can do for each other? Who is the neighborhood police chief, shepherd, chef, party planner, etc.?

3 When I say the word "hospitality," is there a story or event that comes to mind from your life that illustrates the meaning of that word for you—that you would be willing to share with us?

4 Glance over the comments Max and Denalyn made that are noted on page 35, plus any notes you may have taken. What points stuck with you?

5 Which one of the following words they used best describes what you long for home to be?

REST, REFUGE, RECOVERY, EXTENSION OF THE BLOCK, IMPERFECT

6 Which of Max's three hospitable steps do you think would present you with the biggest challenge? Why?

Interview with Max Lucado

Play the conversation between Brett Eastman and Max that provides some additional reflection on the theme of hospitality. Use the following questions to respond:

7 Do you know all your immediate neighbors' names? How do you include them in your prayer life?

8 What example can you offer from your life of a time when someone extended hospitality to you and made a profound difference?

9 What would it take for you to be willing to be on the lookout for something similar to the "dirt pile" that Max ended up helping his neighbor move?

Deeper Bible Study

Your group may want to look at the biblical background of this session's emphasis on neighbors. The Bible is filled with examples of hospitality, which was a social rule in the time of Jesus. And yet neighbors were still a challenge. Two passages illustrate the way Jesus focused on the fact that hospitality wasn't always going to be convenient or easy, but was worth doing anyway!

Mark 12:28–34 "What's the Bottom Line?"

1 What clue do you see in the lawyer's observation of Jesus that made him want to ask his question?

2 Jesus and the lawyer agreed on what was most important. Why do you think Jesus said, "You're almost there, right on the border of God's kingdom"?

3 If the bottom line is loving God and neighbors, what are some of the ways we can do better at this?

Luke 10:25–37 "Who's My Neighbor?"

1 Maybe you've asked this question out of frustration or fear. Jesus answered it with a story. How did the man's response to Jesus' story show that he knew exactly what it meant to be a neighbor? How did the Samaritan demonstrate neighborliness?

2 Why was the neighborliness of the Samaritan an issue for the lawyer? What criteria would you use to decide that someone was not your neighbor?

3   What are some practical things you could do to demonstrate neighborliness to those who live closest to you?

Sharing Together

Suggestions for practical application based on the conversation of the session:

1   Which people on your block would you be willing to invite to your home for some kind of adventure in hospitality?

2   Brainstorm as a group some of the activities that you could host at your home. Note the ones that fit your situation.

3   Write some dates that represent when you plan to put into action some exercise of hospitality in your neighborhood.

Hint for Next Time

We've taken on family and neighbors in the last two sessions. You may be feeling a little overwhelmed at this point. Never fear! Next time, we're going to dive into the significant subject of having fun together. We will be learning how to make room to chill. Don't miss this session; it's not too late to bring a friend.

Notes

SESSION
FOUR
making room to chill

The Story Behind the Call to Chill

Randy is quick to admit that his biggest discovery from the lesson of the *Table* was that he needed to chill out (relax, not refrigerate!). This took a conscious effort, though, because busyness can't just be switched off. We learn to slow down one step at a time. As Randy says, the sense of "climbing out of a hole" that chilling can give us makes it worth pursuing.

Rozanne discovered her own joy of chilling when she realized what a delight it was to relax with other women and share their lives together. Hosting a Bible study for women simply became another opportunity to bring people to the table, not just for physical food, but to enjoy the nourishment of God's Word.

"When Jesus got to the tree, he looked up and said, 'Zacchaeus, hurry down. Today is my day to be a guest in your home.' Zacchaeus scrambled out of the tree, hardly believing his good luck, delighted to take Jesus home with him."
(Luke 19:5–6)

And so, away from the "official duties" of a ministry couple, we find a husband and wife seeking to practice what they preach right where they live. Instead of just encouraging others to go home and reach their neighbors, they are modeling for everyone to see how to live a more grace-filled life.

Coming Together

This fourth time together as a group should have
you fairly relaxed with each other. Here are a few
ideas that will allow you to chill your way into the
session.

1 Just a Minute

As you begin, have everyone stand or raise their
hand. Tell them that most of us have a hard time
actually judging time, even though we seem to
be slaves to it. Make sure no one looks at their
watches, but when they think one minute has
expired, have them sit down. (Make sure there are
no clocks in sight.) What does this little experiment
tell you about time?

2 How Do You Spell RELAX?

Invite each person to describe what it takes for him
or her to relax during a gathering. The underlying
question is: what has to be going on in a group for
you to be completely comfortable?

3 How Do You Do That?

Who would you say has been the best example to
you of what it means to chill, or relax, in life? Have
you ever asked them how they do it? If so, what
did you find out?

Learning Together (notes)

Below are some notable statements made during the video by Randy and Max, followed by Rozanne and her group, and then by Randy. Use these and others you note as you talk together.

_____

_____

_____

_____

_____

_____

_____

_____

_____

"You've probably got a 'To Do' list, but do you have a 'To Be' list?"

"Are you willing to develop and work on a 'To Be' list this year?"

"God and Adam and Eve—they chilled together."

Growing Together

Reflect on some of what you heard and saw during the video segments. Offer your thoughts to the group, using some or all of the following questions:

1 Why do you think it's so hard not to feel guilty when we relax?

2 How did you respond when you heard Max and Randy talking about God giving us permission and encouragment to chill?

3 When you were observing Rozanne and her group, what struck you as significant and engaging about the process?

4 What are some of the specific things that come to mind when Randy talks about having a "To Be" list in life? He mentions the fruit of the Spirit (Galatians 5:22–23). What are those character qualities that God promises to give us?

5 What has changed in your life as a result of making time to chill?

Interview with Randy Frazee

Play the extended discussion conversation between Brett and Randy that reflects more of Randy's thinking on the issue of chilling. Use the following questions to respond:

1 What more did you learn about chilling from Randy and Brett's conversation?

2 What did you think of Randy's point that when we are successful, we soon find we are on a never-ending treadmill to satisfy a mistaken identity of achievement instead of an identity based on how God sees and knows us?

Deeper Bible Study

Your group may want to look at some biblical passages that illustrate the power of chilling.

Luke 15:8–10 "Look What I Found!"

1 The woman lost her coin and then threw a party when she found it. Any excuse will do to gather the neighbors. Invent a holiday!

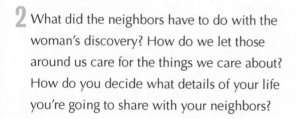

2 What did the neighbors have to do with the woman's discovery? How do we let those around us care for the things we care about? How do you decide what details of your life you're going to share with your neighbors?

3 What was Jesus illustrating by using this story and the other two in Luke 15? What happens in heaven when one of us gets found?

4 The woman did "invent a holiday" for personal reasons. What kinds of holidays might you identify as good reasons to get together? Think beyond the usual suspects: instead of a Super Bowl party, you could have a party two weeks later called a "Football Season Recovery Party."

5 When we think about sharing the gospel with our neighbors, do we tend to think more in terms of "Here's some news I know you don't really want to hear" or in terms of "I can't wait to tell you what I've found that changed my life"?

John 2:1–11 "Here, Taste This!"

1 What was Jesus doing at this wedding? How do you envision him at most social gatherings?

2 What do you think was going on in the relationship between Mary and Jesus? Did the fact that he was about to embark on his public ministry have something to do with reminding his mother that he was no longer at her beck and call? How?

3 Why did Jesus turn the water into wine? What's the significance of him doing instantly (as C.S. Lewis put it) what he does gradually each growing season in producing wine? How did Jesus' miracle help the people chill (relax) at the wedding?

Sharing Together

Suggestions for practical application based on the conversation of this session:

1 How will your priorities be rearranged when you include time to chill in your life? How will the way you use your time and energy have to change?

2 How can the people in your group help you keep on track with more chilling in your life? What do you want them to ask you?

3 Brainstorm a group "To Be" list for a few minutes. Choose at least five of the qualities of being that you long to see more apparent in your life and record them below. Ask God to help you develop these inner sources as you chill these next few months.

Hint for Next Time

We have completed four sessions in our *Making Room For Neighbors* series. We are now at the "seventh-inning stretch" and the best is yet to come. Max and Denalyn will help us finish strong as they share personal stories on how to make room for service. Don't miss this last session. It's a chance to celebrate all that God has done.

Notes

SESSION
FIVE
making room for service

The Story Behind the Project

The house is a neighborhood eyesore. Weeds, an overgrown lawn, and evidence of poor maintenance eventually cause concern from the neighbors. It's the "one bad apple" syndrome. One poorly kept property and the value of the whole neighborhood goes down the drain.

Certain conclusions might be reached about the owner of such a house, and those conclusions might be wrong. In Terri's case, they certainly were. Of all the people in the neighborhood who were upset about the condition of her home, none was more concerned than the owner, Terri. As a suddenly divorced

"That is what the Son of Man has done: He came to serve, not to be served—and then to give away his life in exchange for many who are held hostage."
(Mark 10:45)

mom, her problem wasn't that she couldn't see how her property looked, but that she was almost helpless to do anything about it. Personal, health, and financial issues had left her frozen in place, unable to take the first step toward order.

But Terri lived in a neighborhood where people not only cared about the appearance of the properties, they also cared about the people living in the homes. Terri's predicament became a simple opportunity for a number of neighbors to join forces and do something wonderful for someone who could hardly help herself.

Coming Together

This last study in *Making Room for Neighbors* need not be the last time you meet. Hopefully, members of your group are intentionally gathering their neighbors to chill with one another. In some cases, they are teaming up with their neighbors to make an impact on the wider community. You've got reasons to celebrate! This session will show you how some folks found a way to touch a neighbor's life with (as Jesus put it) "a cup of cold water" in his name. Here are a few ideas you can use to start this session.

1 Chill Report

Who can report a delightful moment of chilling this past week? What about a situation where you saw someone else chilling in an effective way? How would you say relaxing has helped you see things from a new perspective?

2 Global Impact

Have each person place a star anywhere on this map they have visited for more than a day. Share your map with the group. What does this tell you about your group? How does your wealth of experience put you in a position to think about ways you can offer service not only to the people in your backyard, but also around the world?

Roll Tape
DVD
Session 5

Learning Together (notes)

The section below provides you with some open space to write down your reactions, reflections, and resolutions based on the teaching and testimonies. As you listen, write down your thoughts and be prepared to discuss them later.

_____

_____

_____

_____

_____

_____

_____

_____

_____

"There's nothing like working beside people to help you get to know them."

Growing Together

Again, imagine you get to join the conversation between Max and Denalyn. Reflect on some of what you heard and saw during the video segments. Offer your thoughts to the group, using some or all of the following questions:

1 What does the simple "cup of cold water" mean to you? What did Max mean by "don't overcomplicate things"?

2 Describe a time in your life when someone provided you with "a cup of cold water" when you needed it the most.

3 If Randy is right that there's a story behind every front door, then how many people on your block or in your apartment building do you think know your story?

4 What significance do you take away from Max's statement that "God has placed us in our neighborhood"? What reasons might God have had for dropping you in the spot where you live?

Interview with Max Lucado

Play the conversation between Brett and Max that provides some additional reflection on the theme of service. Use the following questions to respond:

1 So, are you more like Max or like Denalyn? What have these sessions caused you to do to overcome points of resistance or hesitation toward your neighbors?

{ }

2 In what ways has this conversation affected your view of service?

{ }

3 What are some "small deeds" you could do to make a big impact on your neighborhood?

{ }

Deeper Bible Study

The Bible is filled with encouragement to us to serve others. Jesus defined his own purpose for coming to earth in terms of service, the kind that was self-sacrificing. The following two passages offer you a start at looking at the central place of service in all that we do as Christians—especially in the places where we live.

John 13:1–17 "Imitating Jesus"

1 What direct reason does John give for why Jesus washed his disciples' feet?

2 What lesson did Peter get taught (again) on this occasion?

3 In verses 12–17, Jesus explained his actions. He didn't surrender his role, but what did he point out to the disciples about the significance of his act of serving them? How did Jesus' attitude counter almost everything that normally happens in the hierarchy of human relationships?

Philippians 2:12–18 "Working it Out"

1 Was Paul trying to get the Philippians to try something new or to keep doing what they already knew they should do—only better? In what ways?

2 In what ways do Paul's instructions mention serving others?

3 How many of your neighbors know you are a Christian? How did they discover that? Do those neighbors who know you're a Christian see that as a positive or negative mark on your life? If God placed you in your neighborhood, how are you living out that placement?

Sharing Together

Suggestions for practical application based on the conversation of the session:

1 What are some simple yet practical projects that you could undertake as a group to offer service to someone in your neighborhood? Take a few minutes to brainstorm a list and then decide which one you will do first. You can call it your Neighborhood Project.

_____

_____

_____

_____

_____

_____

2 What are some personal projects that you have been considering with your spouse, family, or friends related to your immediate neighborhood? Are there any ways the group can help you pull those off?

3 In Session One, you wrote down at least three dreams. How many of those, if any, have come true? Again, is there any way this group could help you reach those dreams this year?

Hint for Next Time

Discuss where you will go as a group from here. Will you continue to meet? What will be your study subject? Where will you meet? Make sure you draw this study to an official close in order to both celebrate what God has done and anticipate what he has yet to do. Finally, share a prayer of gratitude for your time together.

Notes

_____

_____

_____

_____

_____

_____

_____

_____

_____

Appendix

Frequently Asked Questions

1 What do we do on the first night together?

Like all fun things in life—have a party! A "get to know you" coffee, dinner, or dessert is a great way to launch a *Making Room for Neighbors* study. Everyone should bring someone, and more importantly, something to eat. You may want to review the Neighborhood Agreement on page 63 and share the names of a few friends you can invite to join you. But most importantly, have fun before your first official session together.

2 Where do we find new members for our group?

This can be troubling, especially for new groups that have only a few people or for existing groups that lose a few people along the way. We encourage you to pray with your group and then brainstorm a list of people from work, church, your neighborhood, your children's school, family, the gym, and so forth. Then have each group member invite several of the people on his or her list. Another good strategy is to ask church leaders to make an announcement or allow a bulletin insert.

No matter how you find members, it's vital that you stay on the lookout for new people to join your group. All groups tend to go through healthy attrition—the result of moves, releasing new leaders, ministry opportunities, and so forth—and if the group gets too small, it could be at risk of shutting down. If you and your group stay open, you'll be amazed at the people God sends your way. The next person just might become a friend for life!

3 How long will this group meet for?

It's totally up to the group. Most groups meet weekly for at least the first few weeks, but every other week can work as well. However, we strongly recommend that the group try to meet on a weekly basis for a season if at all possible.

This allows for continuity, and if people miss a meeting, they aren't gone for a whole month.

At the end of this study, group members may decide to continue on for another multi-week study. Some groups launch relationships for years to come, and others are stepping stones into another group experience. Either way, enjoy the journey.

4 Can we do this study on our own?

Absolutely! This may sound crazy, but one of the best ways to do this study is not with a full house, but with a few friends. You may choose to gather with others who would enjoy going to the movies or having a quiet dinner, and then walking through this study. "When two or three of you are together because of me, you can be sure that I'll be there" (Matthew 18:20).

5 What if this group is not working for us?

You're not alone! This could be the result of a personality conflict, life stage difference, geographical distance, level of spiritual maturity, or any number of things. Relax. Pray for God's direction, and at the end of this five-week study, decide whether to continue with this group or find another. You don't buy the first car you look at or marry the first person you date, and the same goes with a group. Don't bail out before the five weeks are up, though. God might have you there for a reason you don't see yet. Also, don't run from conflict or judge people before you have given them a chance. God is still working in you too!

6 Who is the leader?

Most groups have an official leader. But ideally, the group will mature and members will rotate the leadership of meetings. We have discovered that healthy groups rotate hosts/leaders and homes on a regular basis. This model ensures that all members grow, give their unique contribution, and develop their gifts. The Holy Spirit and this workbook can keep things on track even when you rotate leaders.

Christ has promised to be in your midst as you gather. Ultimately, God is your leader each step of the way.

7 *How do we handle the childcare needs in our group?*

Very carefully. Seriously, this can be a sensitive issue. We suggest you empower the group to openly discuss solutions. You may try one option that works for a while and then adjust over time. Our favorite approach is for adults to meet in the living room or dining room, and to share the cost of a babysitter (or two) who can be with the kids in a different part of the house. In this way, parents don't have to be away from their children all evening when their children are too young to be left at home.

A second option is to use one home for the kids and a second home (close by or a phone call away) for the adults. A third idea is to rotate the responsibility of providing a lesson or care for the children either in the same home or in another home nearby. This can be an incredible blessing for kids.

Finally, the most common idea is to decide that you need to have a night to invest in your spiritual lives individually or as a couple, and to make your own arrangements for childcare. No matter what decision the group makes, the best approach is to speak openly about both the problem and the solution.

A Neighborhood Agreement

Our Purpose

Our purpose is to transform our spiritual lives by cultivating our spiritual health in a healthy environment. In addition, we agree to the following:

Group Attendance	To give priority to the group meeting. We will call or e-mail if we will be late or absent. (Completing the group calendar will minimize this issue.)
Safe Environment	To help create a safe place where people can be heard and feel loved. (Please, no quick answers, snap judgments, or simple fixes.)
Respect Differences	To be gentle and gracious to people with different spiritual maturity, personal opinions, temperaments, or imperfections. We are all works in progress.
Confidentiality	To keep anything that is shared strictly confidential and within the group; to avoid sharing improper information about those outside the group.
Encouragement for Growth	To be not just takers but givers of life. We want to spiritually multiply our lives by serving others with our God-given gifts.
Welcoming Newcomers	To keep an open chair and share Jesus' dream of finding a shepherd for every sheep.
Shared Ownership	To remember that every member is a minister and to ensure that each attendee will share a small team role or responsibility over time.
Rotating Hosts/Leaders and Homes	To encourage different people to host the group in their homes and to rotate the responsibility of facilitating each meeting. (See the group calendar.)

Our Expectations

- Refreshments/mealtimes _____
- Childcare_____
- When we will meet (day of week) _____
- Where we will meet (place) _____
- We will begin at (time) _____
- We will end at (time) _____
- Date of this agreement _____
- Date we will review this agreement again _____
- Who (other than the leader) will review this agreement at the end of this study_____

Conversation Starters to Use with Your Neighbors

Good questions draw people in and keep a conversation flowing. Be on the lookout for good questions. Below are some suggestions.

1. What's your preferred ice cream flavor? Where do you usually enjoy it?
2. How many brothers and sisters do you have? What is your birth order?
3. Which do you prefer: the hustle and bustle of city life, or the quiet and serenity of country life? Why?
4. What's your all-time favorite meal, and how often do you get to eat it?
5. What's one of your nicknames? What do you prefer to be called?
6. As a child, what was your idea of fun?
7. What's a phrase your parents said to you as a child that you promised yourself you'd never say, but now catch yourself saying all the time?
8. As a kid, what did you want to grow up to be?
9. What's one of your hobbies?
10. What books have made a big impact on you?
11. What was the most recent compliment that surprised and delighted you?
12. What's something about yourself that you hope will never change?
13. Are you more of a rule-breaker or a rule-keeper? Why?
14. Would you describe yourself as an extrovert or an introvert? Explain.
15. What's your dream job?
16. What's one of your greatest achievements?
17. What one word sums up your high school experience? Why?
18. What's the first thing that comes to mind when you hear the word "fun"?
19. What are you a "natural" at doing? What skills have you always had?
20. How often do you eat a leisurely meal with friends?

Memory Verses

Below you will find a suggested memory verse for each of the five sessions in *Making Room for Neighbors*. The practice of memorizing and meditating on God's Word has been proven through the centuries to provide those who do it with a continual source of guidance, inspiration, wisdom, and intimacy with God. God loves it when we intentionally think his thoughts. Feel free to cut out the memory verses and place them in your wallet or purse to review over the next few months.

Session One
Making Room for Life

"Then he [Jesus] said to his disciples, 'The harvest is plentiful but the workers are few. Ask the Lord of the harvest, therefore, to send out workers into his harvest field.'" (Matthew 9:37–38, NIV)

Session Two
Making Room for Family

"Therefore, as we have opportunity, let us do good to all people, especially to those who belong to the family of believers." (Galatians 6:10, NIV)

Session Three
Making Room for Neighbors

"Jesus said, 'The first in importance is, "Listen, Israel: The Lord your God is one; so love the Lord God with all your passion and prayer and intelligence and energy." And here is the second: "Love others as well as you love yourself." There is no other commandment that ranks with these.'" (Mark 12:29–31)

Session Four
Making Room to Chill

"The thief comes only to steal and kill and destroy; I have come that they may have life, and have it to the full." (John 10:10, NIV)

Session Five
Making Room for Service

"That is what the Son of Man has done: He came to serve, not to be served— and then to give away his life in exchange for many who are held hostage." (Mark 10:45)

Prayer and Praise Report

If you are comfortable doing so, briefly share your prayer needs with your group. Then gather in smaller groups of two to four to pray for each other. Use the space below to keep track of specific requests.

	Prayer Requests	Praise Requests
SESSION ONE		
SESSION TWO		
SESSION THREE		

	Prayer Requests	Praise Requests
SESSION FOUR		
SESSION FIVE		

Leader Notes

Hosting an Open House

If you're starting a new group, try planning an "open house" before your first formal group meeting. Even if you only have two to four core members, it's a great way to break the ice and to consider prayerfully who else might be open to join you over the next few weeks. You can also use this kick-off meeting to hand out study guides, spend some time getting to know each other, discuss each person's expectations for the group, and briefly pray for each other.

A simple meal or good desserts always make a kick-off meeting more fun. After people introduce themselves and share how they ended up at the meeting (you can play a game to see who has the wildest story!), have everyone respond to a few icebreaker questions: "What was the best meal you ever had and why?" "What is your favorite vacation memory?" Next, ask everyone to tell what he or she hopes to get out of your time together. You might want to review the Neighborhood Agreement and talk about each person's expectations and priorities.

Finally, set an open chair (maybe two) in the center of your group and explain that it represents someone who would enjoy or benefit from this group who may live right down the street. Ask people to pray about whom they could invite to join the group over the next few weeks. Don't worry about ending up with too many people—you can always have one discussion circle in the living room and another in the dining room after you watch the lesson. Each group could then report prayer requests and progress at the end of the session.

You can skip this kick-off meeting if your time is limited, but you'll experience a huge benefit if you take the time to connect with each other in this way.

Top 10 Ideas for Leading and Hosting

Congratulations! You have responded to the call to help be a shepherd for Jesus' flock. There are few other tasks in the family of God that surpass the contribution you will be making. As you prepare to lead—whether it is one session or the entire series—here are a few thoughts to keep in mind. We encourage you to read these and review them with each new discussion leader before he or she leads.

1 **Remember that you are not alone.** God knows everything about you, and he knew that you would be asked to lead your group. Even though you may not feel ready to lead, this is common for all good leaders. Moses, Solomon, Jeremiah, and Timothy were all reluctant to lead. God promises, though, "Never will I leave you; never will I forsake you" (Hebrews 13:5, NIV). Whether you are leading for one evening, for several weeks, or for a lifetime, you will be blessed as you serve.

2 **Don't try to do it alone.** Pray right now for God to help you build a healthy leadership team. If you can enlist a co-leader to help you lead the group, you will find your experience to be much richer. This is your chance to involve as many people as you can in building a healthy group. All you have to do is ask people to help—you'll be blessed by the response.

3 **Just be yourself.** If you won't be you, who will? God wants to use your unique gifts and temperament. Don't try to do things exactly like another leader; do them in a way that fits you! Just admit it when you don't have an answer and apologize when you make a mistake. Your group will love you for it—and you'll sleep better at night.

4 **Prepare for your meeting ahead of time.** Review the session and the leader's notes, and write down your responses to each question. Pay special attention to exercises that ask group members to do something other than engage in discussion. These exercises will help your group live what the Bible teaches, not just talk about it. Be sure you understand how an exercise works, and bring any necessary supplies (such as paper or pens) to your meeting.

If the exercise employs another item in the book (such as the three-month calendar on the inside cover), be sure to look over that item so you'll know how it works. Finally, review the Introduction to this book on pages 8–12 so you'll remember the purpose of each section in the study.

5 **Pray for your group members by name.** Before you begin your session, go around the room in your mind and pray for each member by name. You may want to review the prayer list at least once a week. Ask God to use your time together to touch the heart of every person uniquely. Expect God to lead you to whomever he wants you to encourage or challenge in a special way. If you listen, God will surely lead!

6 **When you ask a question, be patient.** Someone will eventually respond. Sometimes people need a moment or two of silence to think about the question. If you show that the silence doesn't bother you, it will be less likely to bother others.

After someone responds, affirm the response with a simple "Thanks" or "Good job." Then ask, "How about somebody else?" or "Would someone who hasn't shared like to add anything?" Be sensitive to new people or reluctant members who aren't ready to say, pray, or do anything. If you give them a safe setting, they will blossom over time.

7 **Provide transitions between questions.** When guiding the discussion, always read aloud the transitional paragraphs and the questions. Ask the group if anyone would like to read the paragraph or Bible passage. Don't call on anyone, but ask for a volunteer, and then be patient until someone begins. Be sure to thank the person who reads aloud.

8 **Break up into small groups each week, or they won't stay.** If your group has more than seven people, we strongly encourage you to have the group split into circles of three or four people during the more intimate sections of the study. With a greater opportunity to talk and pray in a small circle, people will connect more with the study, apply what they're learning more quickly, and ultimately